GETTING INTO

Psy y

THIRD ED

TROTMAN

First published in 1994; Second edition 1996
This third edition published in 1999
by Trotman & Company Ltd,
2 The Green, Richmond, Surrey TW9 1PL

British Library Cataloguing in Publication Data
A catalogue record for this book is available from the British Library.

ISBN 0 85660 458 5

Printed and bound in Great Britain
by Creative Print & Design (Wales)

CONTENTS

Preface *v*
Glossary of terms *vi*
About this book *vii*

1 **Introduction to psychology** 1
How long is a piece of string? 1
Now you see it... 3
It's not what you say, it's the way that you say it 4
How do children think? 5
Why is psychology so popular? 6

2 **Degree programmes in psychology** 8
General or specialised? 8
Single subject, joint or modular? 9
Full time or sandwich? 9
Degree course content 10

3 **Careers in psychology** 13
1 Professional psychology 13
2 Related careers 18
3 Options unrelated to psychology 18
What about employability? 19

4 **Applications: Section 10 of the UCAS form** 21

5 **Succeeding in your interview** 23
General hints for interviews 23
Finding the facts 25
Questions you need to ask 25

Appendix: The universities & colleges 28

Further information & reading list 68
British Psychological Society 68
General university guides 69
Psychology texts 69

PREFACE

Over the past few years the number of applicants for degree courses in Psychology has increased enormously and, as part of MPW's work of advising would-be students on their choice of higher education, we have gathered together a huge amount of information on psychology courses.

With the encouragement of Trotman & Company this information was brought together in the form of a guide a few years ago, and has proved so popular, and is such a changing field, this book is now in its third edition.

We are grateful to Judy Leung who read Psychology at Bath University for her research into this topical area of careers advice, and to Ben Ball who has revised and updated the material for this new edition. I hope that this guide will be of use wherever eager sixth-formers want to know more about getting into psychology.

MPW
June 1999

GLOSSARY OF TERMS

It is important to distinguish between the role of the psychologist and other professionals carrying out related work.

Psychiatrist

A medically trained doctor who chooses to specialise in mental health by taking the membership examinations of the Royal College of Psychiatry. As a consequence of their medical training, psychiatrists can prescribe drug treatments. They will often work as part of a team with clinical psychologists.

Psychotherapist

Works with both individuals and groups to provide long-term therapy. They will often encourage clients to reflect on their past experience and early development. In theory, graduates of any subject can become a psychotherapist by taking a lengthy training programme of supervised clinical practice and seminars and, in addition, undergoing personal therapy themselves.

Psychoanalyst

Bases his or her work on Freudian theory and tries to unearth the influence of the unconscious on clients' behaviour. Psychoanalysts work with individual clients in private practice rather than in paid employment. As with psychotherapy, the training period of at least four years includes the process of personal analysis.

ABOUT THIS BOOK

Deciding what to study after A-levels is a daunting task. There are already numerous books, guides and leaflets available to help you make your choice. So, why bother to write yet another? *Getting into Psychology* is, as the title suggests, specifically for people wanting to do psychology at degree level. We hope it provides a clear and concise introduction to a subject which relatively few students do at school. It contains information on: entry requirements, the length and content of the various courses on offer, a little about the actual university psychology departments and some guidelines on filling in section 10 of your UCAS form and preparing for an interview. If, after reading the following chapters, your decisions have been eased in any way, we will have achieved our goal.

It is intended to complement, not replace, existing publications, many of which are included in the reading list at the end of the guide.

Details of entry requirements, courses, campus facilities, etc are constantly changing and, although the details in this guide are correct at the time of going to press, it is essential to check with UCAS and/or particular universities if you have any queries.

Chapter 1
INTRODUCTION TO PSYCHOLOGY

Psychology is an increasingly popular subject of study with nearly 100 higher education institutions offering degree-level courses in the subject either as free-standing degree programmes in their own right or as modules in other combined programmes. Despite this growth in student places, there are still, however, some popular misconceptions about the content of degree programmes. They do not offer students the chance to spend three years studying the works of Freud. Nor do they enable you to see into other people's innermost thoughts.

On the contrary, psychology is taught as a scientific subject and students spend most of their time studying the results of research into human behaviour and the theories which are based on experimental findings. The aim of this introductory chapter is to give you an insight into some of the typical psychological research findings you are likely to study in the course of a degree programme.

HOW LONG IS A PIECE OF STRING?

In 1955, the psychologist Solomon Asch set up an experiment in which he sat a group of people around a table and asked them, in turn, to state which of three lines (drawn on one card) was the same length as the single line shown on another card. So, A, B or C?

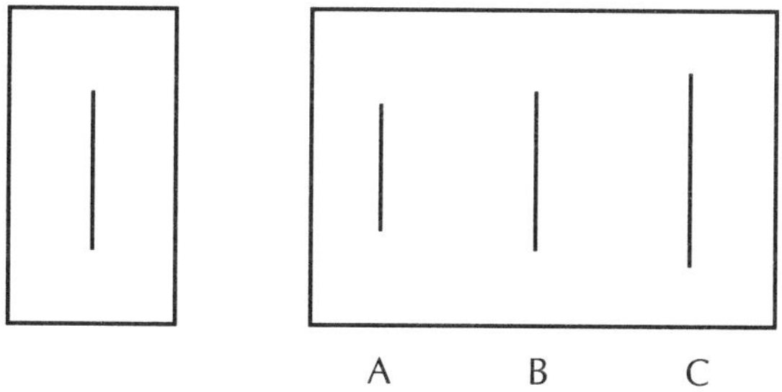

The answer is not as easy as it seems. In fact, the experiment was arranged so that all but one of the group were told beforehand to give the same, but incorrect, answer (ie A). The other person, the 'naive subject' who was not in on the act, was placed to answer last. Surprisingly, despite the simplicity of the task, the naive subject often gave the same wrong answer as his or her companions, preferring to conform than to stand out. It's amazing what peer pressure can do! 'So what?' I hear you cry, 'No one goes round asking complete strangers to judge the lengths of lines.'

In subsequent experiments, Asch found that the naive subject's response often varied with the composition of the group. If one other person deviated from the general consensus (even if he or she gave the other wrong answer), then the subject usually gave the correct response. If the subject was allowed to write his or her judgement on paper, the answer was always right and, if someone left the room before responding, the subject felt able to give the right answer (assuming, no doubt, that the absent person would have given the correct reply).

It seems, therefore, that a person's expressed thoughts and opinions are not necessarily what he or she secretly believes. The study was deliberately designed to be simple and unlike anything the naive subjects had previously experienced so that they could not refer to past events to guide their behaviour. In addition, there was no risk of some members being thought of as more 'expert' than others in the field of judging line length!

Therefore, if peer pressure could have such a profound effect in this simple task, imagine the implications for real life situations. Many other researchers did similar studies, finding that the results varied according to factors such as, how the subject rated his or her companions, whether the subject wanted to be accepted by them and wished to conform, or whether the subject felt superior to them and didn't care that they might be ridiculed for deviating from the general judgement, and so on.

NOW YOU SEE IT...

A good deal of experimental research in psychology has centred on the theme of perception in order to explain how we see and hear. One particular challenge facing psychologists was to account for the way visual illusions, such as the Muller-Lyer illusion below, achieve their effect. Why, for example, does the vertical line in A look longer than that in B?

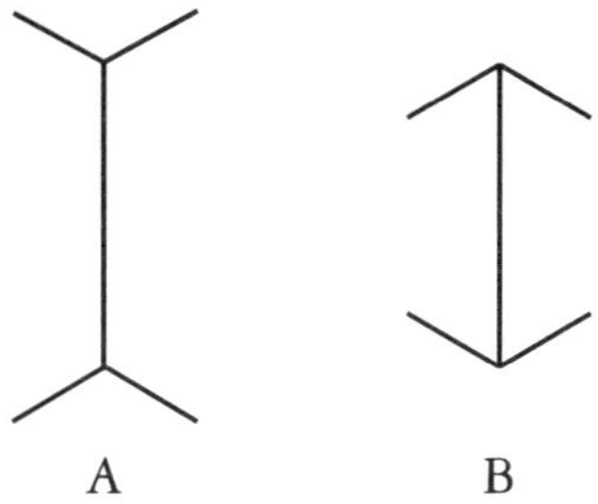

How can the brain interpret one set of signals in two different ways? One explanation, offered by a researcher called RL Gregory, suggests that the context in which a signal is seen, as well as one's expectations, are both highly influential in the interpretation of sensory signals (visual, audio and tactile). So, if a signal is incomplete, the gaps are filled by what you expect to see, hear or touch, rather than with what is really there. Research into this can provide valuable information on how perception normally happens and allows exploration of what can go wrong.

Again, there are far-reaching applications of the findings of such work. For example, if perception is influenced by suggestion and expectation, the gaps filled by the probable rather than the definite, surely the same is true of memory, raising the question: 'How reliable is eye-witness evidence?' Then there is the issue of artificial perception and intelligence – can a computer think or is it only as clever as the person who programmes it?

Coming back to the lines, the way they appear is all to do with perspective. We are fooled into thinking that the 2D image on paper is a 3D phenomenon. Think of it in terms of a room. The vertical line in A is the far corner of a room and the diagonal lines represent the ceiling coming towards us. The diagram in B also shows the corner of a room, but this time it's the corner closest to us and the diagonal lines are the ceiling receding into the distance. Now, because the line in A represents a corner further away from us than the line in B, our brain amplifies the image falling on the retina of the eye to compensate for the extra distance, making it look longer than the line in B which is not amplified. It's a bit like when you see a car on the horizon: you know that it looks tiny because it is a long way away and your brain makes the necessary adjustment to make it look 'car-sized'.

Therefore, perspective is normally useful to us, but the illusion arises if we use it when it is not needed (line A is NOT further away than line B). It's complicated but it is a handy tool to have; artists, architects and designers all make use of it when depicting 3D things on a flat piece of paper. Perspective is, however, a learned process. People who are deprived of seeing things in the distance – like some forest-dwelling tribes and those held in captivity for long periods – do not see things in perspective and, to them, both lines would look the same length.

IT'S NOT WHAT YOU SAY, IT'S THE WAY THAT YOU SAY IT

Verbal communication is interesting for two reasons. First, in association with the theories of speech: how do we learn? Do we plan exactly what to say before we say it or do we put the finishing touches to grammar and word order as we go along? (Think about the errors of speech, how we stumble over words, say them in the wrong order and then go back to make corrections, how we use plural verbs with a singular subject, and so on.) Those 'ums' and 'ahhhs' so common in everyday speech are pauses that allow planning time for the next segment of the sentence.

Second is the way a message is given. How, and by whom, it is delivered can be as influential as its content. For example, is it more effective to speak first or second in a debate? Will the voters remember more of what they heard first or of what they heard most recently? Indeed, do political campaigns really make a difference to voting behaviour? Is an attractive person more likely to be believed than a less attractive one? If not, perhaps spending so much money on media image is a waste of time. Maybe a voter will assure each party that it can rely upon his or her support, reserving his or her choice for the privacy of the polling booth (remember Asch and his lines)? The list is endless!

HOW DO CHILDREN THINK?

Swiss psychologist Jean Piaget earned international renown for his studies of children's intellectual development. As a result of his observations of their behaviour, he suggested that each child goes through a sequence of developmental stages up to the age of 12. One particular experiment characterised the child's thought processes at an early stage of their development and illustrates the process Piaget referred to as 'conservation'.

During the experiment he showed a child two identical glasses with equal amounts of liquid and asked the child to agree that they were the same in volume. Piaget then poured the liquid into glasses of different sizes, one tall and thin and the other shorter and wider than the other. Typically the pre-school child no longer agreed that the two

glasses contained equal amounts of liquid, arguing that the taller glass had more liquid. At this stage in its cognitive development, the child centres on the appearance of the objects rather than accepting that the volume of the liquid is conserved.

This is simply one example of a lifetime of research into child development undertaken by Piaget. Some of his findings have been challenged by later researchers who have shown that infants in particular are more skilled, cognitively, than Piaget suggested. His ideas, however, have proved highly influential in showing the way that children's thought processes develop over time and have been widely incorporated into the training of teachers and educational psychologists.

If you are keen to find out more, there is a huge array of excellent introductory books on psychology, which will provide an overview of the subject as a whole.

WHY IS PSYCHOLOGY SO POPULAR?

Overall, then, why is psychology such a popular subject for a first degree? There are several reasons.

- Potential students are attracted to a subject that gives them insights into human behaviour and most students of psychology have a basic interest in people.
- It is a particularly attractive subject for mature students who may have already have touched on the subject during previous training. Business managers, nurses and social services staff may well have been introduced to some of the basic concepts in psychology and want to learn more.
- Psychology is a subject that can be seen to span both arts and science subjects. It attracts students who have broadly based interests and abilities, who do not want to be seen as either an 'arts' or a 'science' person.

- Finally, although the subject of psychology has been studied at university level for a century – the first professor of psychology was appointed in 1919 – it is still seen as a comparatively 'new' subject and because of the volume of research carried out around the world, students will be studying a subject in which the boundaries of knowledge are constantly changing.

What is more, as a result of the diverse applications of psychology in, for example, healthcare, sports psychology and organisational development many new and exciting work opportunities are being created.

Chapter 2
DEGREE PROGRAMMES IN PSYCHOLOGY

When choosing a degree course in psychology there are several points to bear in mind. First, degree programmes will vary in their emphasis. Some will offer a general but comprehensive grounding in the subject. Others will tend to specialise in one branch of psychology. Secondly, admission to courses is usually open to students irrespective of the A-level subjects or other qualifications they have studied. However, some courses which lead to a Bachelor of Science (BSc) degree in psychology may favour students with science subjects, because of the scientific or experimental nature of the degree course and the ancillary or minor subjects you may be expected to take.

Degree programmes leading to a Bachelor of Arts (BA) degree may look favourably at applicants with arts A-level subjects. The distinction between the two is an important one, because the titles of the awards may not only reflect differences in main course content but also in the choice of subsidiary courses you can take. Those studying for science-based courses may have option choices in neuroscience or physiology whereas those on arts-based programmes may have options in social or developmental psychology.

GENERAL OR SPECIALISED?

Not all first degree programmes in psychology have the same aims. Some are intended to be general in nature, giving a broad and comprehensive overview of all aspects of psychology. Others, by contrast, will attempt to give a special emphasis to one aspect of the subject. You will soon see from the course listings which follow whether a course has a general or specific emphasis. Examples of specialised courses include : Applied, Experimental, Occupational and Social. There can be some benefits in completing this kind of degree particularly if you already know that this aspect of psychology interests you. On graduation, it may also enable you to gain advanced recognition by the relevant professional group or division of the British Psychological Society.

SINGLE SUBJECT, JOINT OR MODULAR?

Most university departments of psychology will offer a single Honours degree in the subject which means that your principal subject is psychology but that you may have to study other minor subjects in addition, which carry less weight in terms of marks and assessment. In addition, there are numerous examples of joint Honours degrees in which you study psychology and one other subject to the same level. Examples include Psychology and Management, Psychology and Mathematics, Psychology and Sociology. This kind of programme enables you to study two subjects in depth, but you may need to check whether the overall workload is slightly higher than studying for a single Honours degree.

By contrast, modular degrees offer a range of different subject modules often linked by a unifying theme. Often called 'combined degrees' they are typically provided by institutes and colleges of higher education and enable students to study psychology alongside other subjects in the social sciences or humanities. With joint degrees, and combined degrees in particular, it is important for applicants to check to see if the degree course is recognised by the British Psychological Society and gives the Graduate Basis for Registration. Without this, it will be difficult to qualify professionally.

FULL TIME OR SANDWICH?

Most degree courses in psychology are full time and last for three years, but some last four years, particularly those in Scotland where it takes four years to gain an Honours degree. A small number of programmes, called sandwich courses, give students the chance to spend their third year on practical placements in companies or with different psychological services or agencies. Students then return to their university for their final year of study.

Although sandwich courses last four years, they can provide students with a valuable opportunity to gain first-hand experience which not only helps them to develop new skills but also to make decisions about which career path to take when they graduate. In one or two instances courses have a 'year abroad' option and arrange for students to spend a year studying at a university outside the UK, in Europe or North America for example.

DEGREE COURSE CONTENT

Most degree courses offer a broad-based introduction to the subject to allow for the fact that many students will not have studied psychology before. This will be followed by increasing specialisation and advanced study as the programme progresses.

First Year

In the first you will be offered introductory courses in different aspects of psychology as well as those in research methods, statistics and the use of information technology. You will hear about some of the key debates in the field of psychological research. For example, how far is human behaviour learned or inherited?

Second Year

Courses in year 2 will build on and extend subjects studied in the first year. You may also have to complete a series of laboratory or experimental classes to give you a practical insight into psychological research methods. The results of your second year assessment may well count towards your final degree result.

Third/Final Year

In the final year of a degree programme, students usually have the opportunity to choose modules or options that interest them, options which typically reflect the research interests of the staff in the Department of Psychology concerned. At the same time students will invariably undertake a major dissertation, based on a research project of their own choosing. This is a significant piece of work and the choice of topic may well have some direct relevance to a student's future career choice.

Definitions

For potential students who have not studied psychology before, the following definitions may be helpful in knowing what might be covered in different course modules:

Cognitive psychology covers the relationship between the brain and human behaviour. It includes the study of memory, thinking and problem-solving.

Clinical and abnormal psychology concerns the symptoms, classification and theories of different forms of mental illness.

Developmental psychology is the study of the process of human growth and development from birth to adulthood.

Neuropsychology looks at the way the central nervous system operates in relation to the sensory processes – seeing and hearing, in particular.

Psycholinguistics involves the interface between psychology and language, its acquisition and structure.

Psychometrics is the measurement of attributes such as aptitude or personality using psychological tests.

If you want to find out more, you can read one of the introductory textbooks designed for first year undergraduates. As well as the topics listed above you may find that a first degree in psychology will also cover some or all of the following:

- social psychology
- language acquisition
- individual differences and psychological testing
- statistics and experimental methods.

Entry Grades

As with other degree subjects, the grades required for entry to degree courses in psychology vary from one university to another. Typically, the older established universities may ask for grades BBB at A-level or their equivalent. By contrast, some of the newer universities may have slightly lower entry requirements. Given the statistical component of most degree courses admissions tutors will also expect applicants to have a reasonable pass grade in GCSE Mathematics.

Further details about the grades required by different universities can be found in some of the listing in the Appendix (page 28).

Chapter 3
CAREERS IN PSYCHOLOGY

There are essentially three main career routes for those who complete a degree course in psychology:

1. To train as a professional psychologist by completing several years of further study and training at postgraduate level.
2. To enter work or postgraduate training which builds on or relates to knowledge gained during a psychology degree programme.
3. To find a graduate-level career which is unrelated to psychology but which may reflect your particular skills and interests.

The three routes are outlined in more detail below to give you an idea of what you might expect after three or four years of study.

1 PROFESSIONAL PSYCHOLOGY

Fewer graduates than you might expect follow this route. In order to qualify as a professional psychologist your degree course must give you the Graduate Basis for Registration (GBR) of the British Psychological Society. This is normally gained by following a course that is accredited by the Society.

Once they meet that condition, graduates will then have to start on a sometimes lengthy period of postgraduate study and practical experience to qualify for Chartered Status to enable them to practise professionally. The main professional career routes are described below.

Clinical Psychology

This is the largest specialism in professional psychology. Working mainly in the National Health Service, clinical psychologists work with clients of all ages by assessing their needs, providing therapy and carrying out research into the effects of different therapeutic methods. Their clients may be otherwise normal people who may have one of a range of problems such as drug dependency, emotional and interpersonal problems or particular learning difficulties. The clinical psychologist's role is not to be confused with that of the psychiatrist (see glossary of terms).

Entry to training programmes is highly competitive and you will need a good pass in your degree as well as relevant work experience. This can be of two kinds – either work experience in some aspect of clinical care or community work or experience as a psychology assistant working alongside existing clinical psychologists in a health authority. Vacancies for assistants occur quite frequently, but after working in this role there is no guarantee of gaining entry to a professional training programme which takes a further three years and leads to a Doctoral degree. This final stage of professional training can either take the form of full-time study at a university coupled with practical experience or an in-service training programme with a health authority.

Occupational Psychology

In comparison with other professional groups, occupational psychologists can work for a variety of employers and can be employed in a number of different roles. In government departments such as the Department for Education and Employment and the Ministry of Defence psychologists can be involved in research or advisory work on the most effective ways of selecting, training and employing personnel. In the Disability Service they assess individual clients and advise on the kind of work and training which might suit them.

By contrast, in business consultancies, psychologists could be involved in the development of new psychological tests or in the design and delivery of company training programmes on topics such as team building. In large companies, occupational psychologists might introduce new systems for staff training and development, while in applied research they could find themselves working alongside engineers on the design of the interface between equipment and its potential user. In short, there are many potential areas of employment and freelance work. To qualify for Chartered Status in this field, psychology graduates need to complete a specialist postgraduate course lasting one year and in addition have three years' supervised work experience.

Educational Psychology

Educational psychologists are experts in child and adolescent development. They work mainly for local education authorities and liaise with teachers and parents in identifying and assessing pupils and students with particular learning difficulties. These can range from dyslexia to disruptive classroom behaviour. Educational psychologists may not be concerned with the treatment of individual problems, but will act in a diagnostic, advisory and consultancy role. The referral of children with special educational needs to special schools is a typical example of a situation in which an educational psychologist's advice would be sought. To qualify for this specialism requires a lengthy period of further study, training and experience.

Different arrangements apply in Scotland, where educational psychologists do not need teaching experience, but in England and Wales psychology graduates are required to complete a one-year course of teacher training and have two years' teaching experience before starting a postgraduate course in Educational Psychology. This is then followed by one year of supervised practice, making it the longest qualification period of any psychology specialism. All this will change, however, in 2001 when the pattern of qualification will resemble that for clinical psychologists.

Forensic Psychology

Often known as criminological psychologists, those in this professional group work mainly in the Prison Service, assessing prisoners in terms of their rehabilitation needs but also in terms of their level of risk. The assessment is usually based on psychometric test results and clinical interviews. In addition, forensic psychologists carry out research and put in place treatment programmes to change offending behaviour and often work with groups of offenders to achieve this aim. Some psychologists in this grouping may also appear in court proceedings to give an expert view on, for instance, the mental state of defendants.

Once again, the qualification period is three years and this comprises study for a postgraduate Masters programme, recognised by the British Psychological Society, along with supervised work experience.

Psychologists in lecturing and research

Academic staff in universities and colleges of higher education will combine teaching activities, such as delivering lectures and running seminars and tutorials, with a commitment to carry out research. Their task is to keep up to date with the latest research findings in their particular area of expertise. They will spend a considerable amount of time making applications for research funding and, once the research is completed, writing journal articles to publish their findings. Entry to academic posts in psychology is very competitive. Lecturers in higher education are not required to have a teaching qualification but those applying for lecturing posts will be expected to have a PhD and to have some published research. Lecturing posts in psychology may also arise in colleges of further education.

For psychology graduates who want to teach in schools the situation is problematic because the subject is not part of the National Curriculum. On balance it is easier for graduates to gain a place on a one-year certificate course to teach at Primary level, but even here different course centres will have their own views about whether to admit psychology graduates who will need to prove that they have the academic interests and experience to equip them for the role of primary teacher.

How to become a professional psychologist

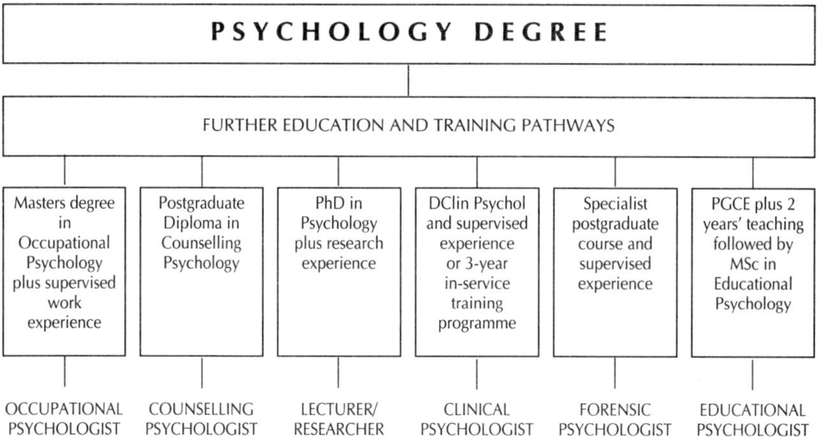

Other professional-level options

A number of emerging specialisms in professional psychology represent small but growing areas of employment. Health psychology involves the application of psychological methods to the study of behaviour related to physical health and illness. It is primarily a research role with little client contact but a focus on healthcare delivery and interventions designed to promote health. One typical area of research would be, for example, the relationship between lifestyle and health. To qualify for this field of work, entrants need to complete a relevant postgraduate course and have two years' supervised experience.

Sports psychology is another new field but there are few full-time jobs and the psychologists involved often lead a portfolio career combining consultancy with lecturing or training.

Counselling psychologists work with individual clients to help them in the processes of overcoming personal problems, improving relationships or the circumstances in which they find themselves. Counselling psychologists can work in community mental health, in large employing organisations, colleges or universities or, as is typically the case, in private practice. To qualify for this professional role, psychology graduates need to take a three-year Diploma in Counselling Psychology which combines practical experience with academic study.

2 RELATED CAREERS

There are several occupations for which a first degree in psychology is a useful entry qualification because of the particular knowledge or skills it provides. For example, an understanding of individual behaviour and social development is highly relevant to careers in teaching and social work. The study of statistical methods and the analysis and interpretation of statistical results can be useful in social and market research, especially when examining the results of large-scale surveys. Any insights psychology students gain into the nature of individual ability and aptitudes, and the ways these can be measured, will provide a foundation for a career in the assessment and selection of personnel. Knowledge you may acquire about physiological and cognitive psychology can be applied in ergonomics, or human factors design, as it is sometimes called. Yet again, an interest in other people's behaviour or personality may well provide the basis of careers which require an element of counselling or interpersonal helping.

By looking carefully at the content of degree programmes, the research interests of lecturing staff and specialist module options which might be available, you will soon begin to see if the course is pointing its students towards a particular career direction in applied psychology.

3 OPTIONS UNRELATED TO PSYCHOLOGY

Many graduates in psychology will choose not to apply the knowledge they have gained from their degree course, but, instead, will use the skills they have gained in a wide range of other graduate-level careers.

Approximately 40% of all graduate job vacancies in the UK are open to graduates irrespective of their degree subject. With a degree in psychology, therefore, it is quite possible to train as an accountant or a solicitor, enter general management, become a journalist or work in information technology. Much will depend on your particular interests and the skills you have developed.

In studying psychology students are often surprised by the number of different skills they develop and which they can use in their work after graduating:

- Information seeking and research skills – the ability to search databases and employ experimental methods.
- Analytical skills – the ability to think critically and weigh the evidence from different research findings.
- Numeracy – the ability to interpret statistical data and to assess the reliability of experimental results.
- IT skills – the ability to use software packages for data analysis and psychological measurement.

These are in addition to the skills that most higher education students will acquire such as the written communication skills developed in essay and report writing or the verbal communication skills used in group projects or seminar discussions and making presentations. As you can see, a psychology degree programme may help you to develop a broad range of skills which you can apply in the workplace, but you may need to make this apparent to potential employers.

WHAT ABOUT EMPLOYABILITY?

It should be clear from the above outline of graduate opportunities that psychology is not a highly vocational degree course such as architecture or dentistry. As a subject of study it does not lead automatically to one particular kind of job. In many ways it can be seen as a semi-vocational course giving students the option of applying their subject knowledge if they choose. A key question for potential applicants to higher education courses, therefore, concerns the overall job prospects for graduates in this kind of subject. An answer is provided by the employment statistics that are collected each year by careers services. The table below reveals the proportions of newly qualified psychology graduates in 1997, from all universities, who entered work and further study.

As you will see, over 60% of psychology graduates went directly into employment and a further 22.5% progressed to further full-time study and training – the majority undertaking postgraduate courses at Master's level.

The 'not available' category consists very largely of graduates who are taking 'time off' to travel to other countries after their degree.

Psychology graduates 1997	**per cent**
1 Entering employment	60.0%
2 Going on to further study	22.5%
3 Not available for work, etc	5.7%
4 Believed unemployed	8.1%
5 Seeking work or further study but not unemployed	1.1%

Total survey response – 5003 graduates

Most universities produce their own employment statistics and if you have a particular university in mind when making your UCAS application, you may like to ask to see the employment data relating to its past graduates in psychology.

Chapter 4
APPLICATIONS: SECTION 10 OF THE UCAS FORM

For general advice on completing your UCAS form, see another book in this series: *How to Complete Your UCAS Form*, written by Tony Higgins, Chief Executive of UCAS.

This chapter is designed to help you plan **Section 10**: your personal statement. This is the only chance you get to prove that, on paper, you deserve a place, or at least an interview, at the universities of your choice. It's vital that you think very carefully about what to say in order to show yourself in the best possible light. It may sound obvious, but they only know what you tell them.

The content of Section 10 is unique to each candidate. There are no rules, as such, but there are recommendations that can be made.

Universities are primarily academic institutions so you must present yourself as a strong bet. The first thing that the admissions tutor wants to know is the strength of your commitment to study. Say clearly why you wish to study for your chosen degree, especially if you haven't studied psychology before. Wanting to work with people, or liking children, is not good enough. Give details of particular areas of study that interest you and say what you hope to get out of researching them at university level.

If there have been certain bits of your A-level pscyhology course which you have enjoyed, say so and tell them why. If you are new to the subject, give examples from newspapers, television events or controversies that have appealed to the psychologist in you. Give examples of your academic interest and explain your reasons for them.

Work experience is useful as it demonstrates a commitment to the subject outside the classroom. If you have had relevant work experience, talk about it on your form. Explain concisely what your job entailed, for example:

> *'During the summer vacation, I am a volunteer at a summer camp for children with learning disabilities. This has been a most valuable work experience and I thoroughly enjoyed working with the children. I have also developed good teamwork and communication skills and have even learnt some sign language!'*

Future plans can also be included, if you have them. Again, be precise and informative. This will demonstrate a breadth of interest in the subject.

At least half of Section 10 should deal with material directly related to your chosen course. Thereafter, use the rest of the page to tell the admissions tutor what makes you who you are. What travel have you undertaken? What music do you like and/or play? What do you read? What sporting achievements do you have? In all these things give details.

> *'Last year I went to France. I like reading and listening to music and sometimes I play football at weekends'*

is weak. A stronger version might read:

> *'Last year I drove through France and enjoyed visiting the chateaux of the Loire. I relax by reading the novels of Stephen King and have hardback first editions of all his books. My musical taste is extremely wide, ranging from Gregorian Chant to Oasis (!) and I would like to continue playing the cello in an orchestra at university. I would also be keen to play in a football team to keep myself fit.'*

Don't expect to fit everything about yourself on this single page and only write things that you are prepared to expand on at interview. The idea is to whet their appetite and to make them want to meet you.

Chapter 5
SUCCEEDING IN YOUR INTERVIEW

Outside Oxford and Cambridge and applications for certain courses, such as medicine, formal interviews are rarely part of the admissions process. They are expensive and time-consuming for both the university and applicants. Nevertheless, sixth formers do worry about interviews and we wanted to include advice on them in this book. It is worth bearing in mind that, for a popular course like pscyhology, you may be able to negotiate a lower offer if you visit the university and speak to the admissions staff. In one sense, that experience is an interview and our general advice should come in useful.

Interviews need not be as dreadful as most candidates fear. There are a number of practical steps that can be taken to reduce the anxiety that inevitably occurs when strangers ask you demanding questions.

GENERAL HINTS FOR INTERVIEWS

- While the number of people conducting the interview and the length of time it takes can vary, all interviews are designed to enable those asking the questions to find out as much about the candidate as they can. It is important, therefore, to engage actively with the process (good eye contact and confident body language help) and treat it as a chance to put yourself across rather than as an obstacle course trying to catch you out.
- Interviewers are more interested in what you know than in what you don't know. If you are asked something you can't answer, say so. To waffle (or worse, to lie) simply wastes time and lets you down. The interviewers will be considering the quality of thought that goes into your answers; they will not expect you to know

everything already. Pauses while you think are perfectly acceptable; don't be afraid to take your time.

- It is likely that one, or more, of the interviewers will be your tutor(s) during your time at university. Enthusiasm for, a strong commitment to, and a willingness to learn your chosen subject are all extremely important attitudes to convey. The people you meet at interview not only have to judge your academic calibre, but also have to decide whether they would enjoy teaching you for the next three to four years.
- An ability to think on your feet is vital. Pre-learned responses never work: they appear glib and superficial and, no matter how apparently spontaneously they are delivered, they are always detectable. Putting forward an answer step by step, using examples and factual knowledge to reinforce your points, is far more professional, even if you are not completely sure of what you are saying. That said, it is also sensible to admit defeat: knowing you are beaten is a more intelligent thing to do than mindlessly clinging to the wreckage of a specious case.
- It is possible to steer the interview yourself to some extent. If, for example, you are asked to comment on something you know little about, confidently replacing the question with another related one shows enthusiasm. Don't waste time in silences that are as embarrassing for the panel as for the candidate.
- Essential preparation includes revision of the personal section of your UCAS form. This may well form the basis of preliminary questions (which are meant to put you at your ease) and if it proves to be a mass of fabrications, the interview is doomed from the start!
- Questions may well be asked about your extracurricular activities. Again, this is to put you at your ease: your answers should be thorough and enthusiastic, but not too long!
- At the end of the interview you are normally given a chance to ask questions of your own. If you have none, say that the interview has covered all the queries you had. It is sensible, though, to have one

or two questions of a serious kind – about the course, the tuition, etc – up your sleeve. Don't ask anything that you could, and should, have found answers to in the prospectus. It is also fine, even desirable, to base a question on the interview itself. This marks you out as someone who listens, is curious and who is keen to learn.

- Above all, make them remember you when they go through a list of 20 or more applicants at the end of the day.

FINDING THE FACTS

Although admissions interviews are not offered routinely by all universities, staff will try to ensure that applicants have a chance to visit the course centre to find out more about the learning environment. Some, for example, will offer group interviews in which a member of staff will lead a discussion about the degree programme, enabling applicants to ask questions about the course. Others will host open days and campus tours which provide applicants the chance of talking to current students about the 'student experience' and viewing the university's facilities.

You should take every opportunity to visit the higher education institutions to which you are applying because, in themselves, prospectus entries will only give you part of the picture. The checklist below will give you an idea of the kinds of questions to ask when you visit a university or college to find out more about a particular course.

QUESTIONS YOU NEED TO ASK

1. About entry

- What additional information is available about the course of study, apart from that in the prospectus?
- What are the aims and objectives of the course?
- What size is the first year intake?

- What entry grades are required? How strictly are these kept to?

2. About study and learning

- Apart from courses in psychology, what other ancillary courses will I need to take?
- What are the class-contact hours for first year students?
- How much time will I have for private study?
- What are the main teaching activities?
- Over the duration of the programme, what proportion of my time will I spend in lectures, seminars, practicals, project work and placements?
- Will it help if I have my own personal computer?

3. About assessment and learning support

- Will I have a personal tutor?
- Are there specific courses in study methods?
- How will my work be assessed?
- Will my first year results count towards the final degree result?
- Are there opportunities to have coaching/mentoring from more experienced students?
- What happens if students fail their first year?

4. About career opportunities and employment

- Do present students receive help in finding part-time work to help pay for the cost of accommodation, fees, etc?
- Is the course recognised by the British Psychology Society, giving the Graduate Basis for Registration?
- Where does the degree course lead in terms of career opportunities and further study?

- What links do lecturers have with employers and practising professional psychologists?
- Are there particular course modules designed to help students with their career decisions?

These questions are largely concerned with the student experience from the perspective of academic study. Intending students are, in addition, likely to have a range of other questions concerning accommodation, finance and the kind of facilities each university has to offer.

Appendix
THE UNIVERSITIES & COLLEGES

Use this section to read a bit more about each of the places on your shortlist. They are arranged alphabetically and each one gives a contact address.

Aberdeen University

The University of Aberdeen, Regent Walk, Aberdeen AB24 3FX
Tel: 01224 272000

Aberdeen offers Psychology as a single Honours degree and joint Honours combining Psychology with Philosophy or Computer Science. The Department takes part in the ERASMUS scheme with other European countries including Germany, Holland and Greece. The Scottish degree structure allows for choice so that students do not need to decide their Honours subject until the end of the second year. Students who wish to pursue a Psychology Honours degree will need to secure a place from the Head of Department who bases the decisions on performance in the first two years (Level 1 and 2). Level 3 (junior Honours) students take courses in methodology, biopsychology, perception and thinking, social psychology, memory, learning, cognition and individual development. Level 4 (senior Honours) students have a choice of options and also prepare a dissertation under staff supervision.

Abertay Dundee University

University of Abertay Dundee, Bell Street, Dundee DD1 1HG
Tel: 01382 308080

BSc Behavioural Sciences involves the integrated study of Psychology and Sociology, strongly focusing on human motivation, behaviour and thought processes. The course is designed to ensure you develop an understanding of both subjects and their impact on each other. Practical problem solving and the gathering and analysis of data are emphasised. If your performance reaches the standard required by the BPS, you may opt to specialise in Psychology in year 3 and exit after year four with an accredited BSc degree in Psychology. Combined degrees include Psychology with Biology or Computing with the major component being psychology. There is a wide range of options in the final year, including cognitive, social, health and clinical psychology, neuropsychology, criminal behaviour and counselling. All final year students submit a supervised project in an area of special interest to them.

Aston

Aston University, Aston Triangle, Birmingham B4 7ET
Tel: 0121 359 3611

You can choose between a three-year programme or a four-year thick sandwich programme which involves a placement year in relevant work experience. Psychology can be studied as a combined Honours option with Biology, Chemistry, Computer Science, French, Public Policy and Management or Social Studies and as a joint Honours in Psychology and Management. The first five weeks of term in the first year include a foundation course giving a general introduction to psychology. This is followed by theoretical psychology, techniques in psychology investigation and the major areas of applied psychology. The final year concentrates on the practical applications of psychological principles. There is a BSc in Psychology and Management which is either a three-year or four-year sandwich course which has been designed to provide an understanding of individual and group behaviour in an organisation's structure. This degree can be a basis for a career in occupational psychology, personnel management or in general management in large organisations.

Bath Spa University College

Bath Spa University College, Newton Park, Bath BA2 9BN
Tel: 01225 875875

Bath Spa offers Psychology as a BA/BSc in combined programmes. It offers a wide range of optional modules allowing Psychology specialists to develop their interests and non-specialists to complement their studies. The course is not BPS approved.

Bath University

The University of Bath, Claverton Down, Bath BA2 7AY
Tel: 01225 826826

This is a four-year course in Psychology with Sociology. This combination allows you to study both the individual's behaviour and the individual in society, social institutions and social structures. Bath's course places an emphasis on social, health, developmental and cognitive psychology. The degree is fully modularised over two semesters per year. Courses comprise 60 credits per year. In Year 1, this is made up of 24 credits in Psychology courses, 12 in methods, 12 in Sociology and 12 in optional subjects. In year two: 24 credits in Psychology, 12 credits in methods, 6 credits for a research project and 18 for options. In year three: 60 credits for placement, and in year four: 18 credits for dissertation and up to 48 credits in Psychology. (Single Honours in Psychology will be available from the year 2000.) The compulsory third-year placement may involve work in research at an academic institution, clinical setting, educational setting, occupational psychology, market research and advertising environments. Several students go abroad for the year. Most placements are unpaid but may be supported by LEA grants where applicable. Dissertations tend to arise from the placement and this year provides valuable work experience which helps in future applications for training and jobs.

Belfast, Queen's University

Queen's University of Belfast, University Road, Belfast,
Northern Ireland BT7 1NN
Tel: 01232 245133

The 1999 subject review of Psychology rated the teaching quality of Psychology at Queen's as 'Excellent', awarding a maximum score of 24. Students follow a three-year degree programme leading to an Honours degree in Psychology (accredited by the BPS). Other options include major and joint Honours degree programmes with many other subjects. The school has extensive computing facilities for students. It has specialised teaching facilities for cognitive, perception, social, developmental, psychobiology, sport and exercise psychology and animal behaviour. The school has close links with local hospitals and schools where many students undertake projects. The school offers opportunities to study a wide variety of topics covering the breadth of the discipline.

Birmingham University

The University of Birmingham, Edgbaston, Birmingham B15 2TT
Tel: 0121 414 2244

There is a large Psychology Department with good purpose-designed facilities and excellent relationships with local hospitals, clinics, industrial companies and departments of local and national government. The school sponsors four research groups: Centre for Research in Cognitive Science, The Midlands Alcohol Research Group, Learning Difficulties Research Group and the Forensic Psychology Consortium. This BSc degree is structured so that for the first two years students follow a common programme in the core areas of Psychology and as finalists are allowed to concentrate on areas of interest. A modular system allows students to take Psychology in combination with selected other subjects.

Bolton Institute

Bolton Institute, Deane Road, Bolton BL3 5AB
Tel: 01204 528851

The Psychology Department is the largest single pathway within the Institute and currently has some 500 students. Psychology may be studied in single, joint, major or minor modes; however, only the single, joint and major modes grant GBR eligibility. The modular degree scheme offers students both mandatory and optional modules. Students study six modules each year (three per semester), which cover all aspects of psychology. In the final year each student conducts an individual research project as well as studying specialised modules.Teaching and research accommodation includes lecture theatres, laboratories, computer suites and a video laboratory.

Bournemouth University

Bournemouth University, Studland House,12 Christchurch Road, Bournemouth, Dorset BH1 3NA
Tel: 01202 524111

It is important today that those who are essentially interested in human behaviour know something about technological systems – how they can be used to help people, and how their design can be improved to this end. People of a more technological inclination need to know something about the people who will use or otherwise be affected by their designs. The three-year BSc Applied Psychology and Computing course examines the interaction of psychological and computing factors in the development of effective, safe and satisfying computer systems.

Bradford University

University of Bradford, Bradford, West Yorkshire BD7 1DP
Tel: 01274 232323

Bradford offers a BA Honours in Interdisciplinary Human Studies which enables you to combine psychology, sociology, philosophy, literature and communication studies. This gives you a broad knowledge of human studies. The course was launched in 1973 and has twice received national commendation. The first two years provide you with the foundations of all the disciplines. In the final year, you may pursue your own interests in greater depth by focusing on one discipline or bringing an interdisciplinary approach to a particular course.

Bristol University

University of Bristol, Senate House, Bristol BS8 1TH
Tel: 0117 928 9000

The Bristol Psychology Department has active links with other departments including child health and sport, exercise and health sciences and with the Burden Neurological Institute. Bristol offers a BSc in the Science and Social Sciences Faculties where psychology components are identical but the choice of first year optional units differs in each case. Joint Honours degrees combine Psychology with Zoology or Philosophy. In the final year, students are encouraged to present reports of projects at an annual South West Area Student Conference.

Bristol, University of West England

University of West of England, Coldharbour Lane, Frenchay, Bristol BS16 1QY
Tel: 0117 965 6261

A BSc in Psychology and Health Science is offered at UWE. This involves the study of psychological, sociological and social policy perspectives on health issues. Practical work is carried out in specialist laboratories for psychology and psychophysiology.

Brunel University

Brunel University, Uxbridge, Middlesex UB8 3PH
Tel: 01895 274000

There are possibilities to study for either a BSc in Psychology or a BSc joint Honours combining Psychology with Sociology or Social

Anthropology. The early stage of the course involves a multidisciplinary approach which is followed by opportunities to specialise. Teaching is heavily influenced by research interests of the staff and the current research field is the Psychology of gender and race. The thin sandwich degree is designed to link academic theory with work experience gained over two separate placements. Students may enter the caring professions, commercial organisations or a public sector organisation. The department helps find suitable placements and most are paid. However, students are encouraged to pursue their own placements, particularly if they would like to go abroad.

Buckingham University

University of Buckingham, Hunter Street, Buckingham MK18 1EG
Tel: 01280 814080

Buckingham offers a Psychology BSc programme taught under the School of Life Sciences. Psychology can be combined with Business Studies, Biology or Computer Science.

Buckinghamshire Chilterns University College

Buckinghamshire Chilterns University College, High Wycombe Campus, Queen Alexandra Road, High Wycombe, Buckinghamshire HP11 2JZ
Tel: 01494 522141

Courses at Buckinghamshire Chilterns are structured on a modular basis over two semesters per year. Psychology can be studied as either single Honours (BSc Psychology) or in combination with the following subjects: Sociology, Philosophy, Criminology, Computing and Sports. The single Honours route is recognised by the BPS and confers the GBR. Psychology is located in a new building with specialist facilities for laboratory work in areas of practical psychology.

Cambridge University

Cambridge Intercollegiate Applications Office, Kellet Lodge
Tennis Court Road, Cambridge CB2 1QJ
Tel: 01223 337733

Psychology is part of a BA in Natural Sciences. The Natural Sciences course is based on general scientific training and allows you to study experimental psychology along with other scientific subjects and to specialise in it in the final year. There is the opportunity to work with leading scientists and within the Medical Research Council's Cognition and Brain Sciences Unit, a leading laboratory in psychology research. Competition for places is tough!

Canterbury Christ Church University College of Higher Education

Canterbury Christ Church University College, North Holmes Road, Canterbury, Kent CT1 1QU
Tel: 01227 782490/782422

Psychology is offered within the Department of Applied Social Sciences as a combined degree (BA/BSc), and is available as a major, joint or minor programme. The psychology programme provides compulsory introductory courses in the first year, and options in years 2 and 3. Courses aim to provide students with a sound discipline as well as equipping them with a wide range of transferable skills. The programme considers students from a variety of academic backgrounds including Access courses, GNVQ and A-level. It is not, however, recognised by the BPS.

Cardiff University

Cardiff University, PO Box 901, Cardiff CF11 3YG
Tel: 01222 874007

The School of Psychology, one of the largest in Britain, has recently been commended in independent assessments for the quality of its research and teaching. The school offers four single (recognised by the BPS for Graduate Membership and Graduate Basis for Registration) and six joint Honours undergraduate degrees. Psychology (3 year) and Applied Psychology (4 year sandwich) are offered as BA or BSc courses. Joint Honours degrees combine Psychology with Criminology, Education, English, Philosophy, Physiology or Sociology. Teaching includes formal lectures combined with practical classes, computer workshops, video demonstrations and small group tutorial work. Students receive a sound foundation in Psychology with the opportunity to focus on their own interests in the final year. Excellent computing and laboratory facilities support the teaching and staff research activities which include family relationships, virtual reality, fault-finding in industry, neuropsychology, the effects of drugs on behaviour, motion perception, face recognition and health psychology.

Central Lancashire University

University of Central Lancashire, Preston PR1 2HE
Tel: 01772 201201

There are two routes through the course leading to either a BSc in Psychology or a BSc in Applied Psychology. Initially students take the same modules and as long as you take the 'Introduction to Applied Psychology' module in the second year, you can delay the decision of which course to follow to the end of that year. Psychology may be studied as a major, joint or minor subject on the combined Honours Programme which allows for flexibility. You can study a language as an option and take part in study opportunities abroad.

Cheltenham & Gloucester CHE

Cheltenham & Gloucester College of Higher Education, PO Box 220, The Park, Cheltenham, Gloucestershire GL50 2QF
Tel: 01242 532700

Psychology is available as a BSc or BA in a major/joint/minor structure. The course begins with a broad overview and concentrates on more specialised areas as the course progresses. The course is currently not recognised by the BPS as conferring the GBR.

Chester CHE

Chester College of Higher Education, Parkgate Road,
Chester CH1 4BJ
Tel: 01244 375444

Chester offers Psychology in single Honours and combined studies degrees, the latter with a wide range of subject combinations in both Arts and Sciences.The degrees are modular and one particular route brings eligibility for GBR with the BPS. Core modules are completed in five semesters and the final semester offers a full choice of optional modules. Stress is placed on practical work and research methods and many modules have an applied slant, ie looking at the contribution of psychology to real world problems, eg educational, organisational, forensic.

City University

City University, Northampton Square, London EC1V 0HB
Tel: 0171 477 8000

Psychology is part of the School of Social Sciences and may be studied as a single BSc Honours degree or combined with Sociology, Economics or Philosophy. This modular degree scheme covers areas in both the social and behavioural sciences. Candidates are asked to make a provisional choice of degree course at the time of application but it is not until the end of the first year that students firmly select their subject of specialisation. The final year options include all major applied and professional areas of psychology.

Coventry University

Coventry University, Priory Street, Coventry CV1 5FB
Tel: 01203 631313

Coventry offers a single Honours BSc in Psychology and a joint Honours combining Psychology with Computer Science or Statistics.

Crewe & Alsager CHE

As for Manchester Metropolitan University

Crewe and Alsager CHE is a Faculty of the Manchester Metropolitan University. Psychology is available as part of a BA (Honours) Applied Social Studies. Part 1 consists of two years of study in which psychology may be combined with units in sociology, philosophy, health studies and special needs (handicap). In Part 2, third year students do a project on their own. Psychology may be combined with exercise physiology and biomechanics as part of a BSc (Honours) Sport and Exercise Science where one studies the variables which influence sports performance, health and exercise. Psychology is also offered as part of a BA (Honours) combined studies where psychology comprises between a half and a third of the degree.

De Montfort University

De Montfort University, The Gateway, Leicester LE1 9BH
Tel: 0116 2551551

De Montfort offers a three-year BSc in Human Psychology. The aim of the programme is to provide students with an insight into the human mind, human abilities and human behaviour. There is also a BSc Psychology of Human Communication degree, which may be a three-year course or a four-year sandwich course. The Human Communication route offers an interdisciplinary approach to the study of communication with an integrated programme of studies built around four core disciplines: psychology, semiotics, linguistics and media studies. The Human Psychology route offers a psychology-based programme for students seeking professional recognition.

Derby University

University of Derby, Kedleston Road, Derby DE22 1GB
Tel: 01332 622222

This three-year BSc in Psychology covers the main theories and methods of contemporary psychology. Courses are offered on a modular basis which includes coursework and exams. Practical work may involve physiological recording of heart rates, food tasting analysis, practical problem solving, video work and memory experiments.

Dundee University

The University, Dundee DD1 4HN
Tel: 01382 223181

Psychology may be taken in the Faculty of Arts and Social Sciences or the Faculty of Science and Engineering. Most Psychology teaching is devoted to courses leading to Honours degrees (four years) and general degrees (three years). The course reflects the research interests of the teaching staff but there is an overriding commitment to present a balanced view of the subject. Laboratory work and experience with micro-computers form an integral part of the practical training.

Durham University

University of Durham, Old Shire Hall, Durham DH1 3HP
Tel: 0191 374 2000

The Department of Psychology offers BA and BSc Honours degrees in Psychology as well as participating in Natural Science, combined Honours and joint Honours degrees. The Department also offers an BSc Honours degree in Applied Psychology at its Stockton campus. Specialised final year options reflect staff research expertise and include cognitive science, developmental psychology, health psychology and neuropsychology at Durham and options directed towards applications of psychology at Stockton.

East London University

University of East London, Romford Road, London E15 4LZ
Tel: 0181 590 7722

Available full-time and part-time and in both the day and evening, the BSc course (BPS accredited) offers a wide choice of specialist study including: psychology of mental health, cognitive neuropsychology, drugs and behaviour, counselling, developing minds, animal behaviour, occupational, evolutionary and forensic psychology. The department also offers postgraduate research courses in all the main areas of professional applied psychology as well as having numerous postgraduate research students.

Edge Hill

Edge Hill CHE, St Helens Road, Ormskirk, Lancs L39 4QP
Tel: 01695 575171

The course leads to a BSc single Honours degree in Psychology (GBR for BPS has been applied for). The three-year full-time programme covers all of the major areas that feature in the BPS qualifying examination: cognitive psychology, social psychology, developmental psychology, biological psychology, personality and individual differences and research methods. In the third year a number of specialist options are available including work psychology, educational psychology, addiction studies, mental health, and sports psychology. Students also undertake a supervised research project in their final year. Psychology is located within the Centre for Studies in the Social Sciences which was rated 'Excellent' for its teaching by HEFCE in their most recent inspection. The course is taught in new purpose-built psychology laboratories. A range of facilities is available including Internet and CD-ROM systems, for example, online journals and abstract databases.

Edinburgh University

The University of Edinburgh, Old College, South Bridge, Edinburgh EH8 9YL
Tel: 0131 650 1000

Single Honours degrees (four years) are available in the Faculty of Social Sciences and in the Faculty of Science and Engineering. There are several joint Honours degrees in which psychology is studied to Honours level along with another subject: artificial intelligence, business studies, linguistics, philosophy or sociology. Psychology can also be studied as part of a three-year ordinary/general degree. In the first three years, all students study a broad range of psychological topics representing the core areas of the discipline. In the fourth year, students can specialise by choosing from a wide variety of options linked to the research expertise of individual members of staff.

Essex University

University of Essex, Wivenhoe Park, Colchester CO4 3SQ
Tel: 01206 873666

Psychology is offered both as a BA and a BSc which builds on the university's strengths in cognitive science, linguistics and social sciences. The course covers the biological basis of behaviour, language, memory, perception, individual differences and child development.

Exeter University

University of Exeter, Northcote House, The Queen's Drive,
Exeter EX4 4QJ
Tel: 01392 263263

The course may be a BSc or a BA; the main syllabus is substantially the same and the choice of Faculty will depend on your A-level subjects and whether you want to complement your degree with Science or Social Science options. Exeter also offers an interdepartmental single Honours BSc in Cognitive Science which works in collaboration with the Department of Computer Science. The emphasis is on computational models of mental processes and the study of language, thought and skills. If one of your A-levels is a modern language, there is the option of spending your third year abroad with LEA support studying psychology at a European university and returning to Exeter for your final year. This involves taking special language courses instead of option courses in the first two years. Selection for non-mature applicants is based mainly on A-level performance and written reports from teachers rather than interviews.

Glamorgan University

University of Glamorgan, Pontypridd CF37 1DL
Tel: 01443 480480

A single Honours BSc is on offer which leads to GBR with the BPS, or as a BA joint Honours degree, combining psychology with a wide range of possible subjects. Glamorgan also offers major/minor routes in psychology. It has good links with sports science and also offer a degree in Sports Psychology.

Glasgow University

University of Glasgow, Glasgow G12 8QQ
Tel: 0141 339 8855

Psychology is offered in the faculties of Arts (MA), Science (BSc) and Social Sciences((MA SocSci), the faculty being determined by the subjects at A-level/Scottish Higher Level. The faculty you enter will also affect the subjects you will study alongside psychology in the first two years of the course. The Honours course is taken over four years and can either be single Honours or joint Honours with a variety of combinations possible. All core areas of psychology are covered, together with statistics and experimental design as well as other topic areas which reflect the expertise and research areas of the staff. The department has a strong research record in various areas, eg perception, neuroscience, addictions, language and cognitive science, and houses both the HCRC (Human Communications Research Centre) and MCG (Multimedia Communications Group). In the recent Teaching Quality Assurance Assessment the department received an 'Excellent'.

Glasgow Caledonian University

Glasgow Caledonian University, Cowcaddens Road, Glasgow G4 0BA.
Tel: 0141 331 3000

The normal length of the course is three years for the degree and four years for a degree with Honours although students who wish to leave the course at the end of Level 2 may be awarded the Diploma in

Higher Education. At Level 3 and 4 students can specialise entirely in psychology or continue to take one module from a discipline other than psychology if they wish. Options are taken from the sciences, social sciences or foreign languages.

Greenwich University

University of Greenwich, The School of Social Sciences, Avery Hill Campus, Avery Hill Road, London SE9 2UG
Tel: 0181 331 8907

Psychology students receive training, which allows them to work as professional psychologists and as generalist graduates in a range of occupations. The BSc (Hons) Psychology is approved as conferring eligibility for Graduate Membership of the BPS. The BSc in Psychology begins with introductory 30 credit units in research methods, individual differences, developmental and social psychology, and cognitive behavioural neuroscience. All students undertake laboratory work including working with computers using the SPSS statistical package.

Hertfordshire University

University of Hertfordshire, College Lane, Hatfield, Hertfordshire AL10 9AB
Tel: 01707 284000

The first year of the BSc Honours Psychology lays a strong foundation in core areas of empirical psychology. Modules in applied developmental and social psychology in the second year underpin a range of final-year option courses which allow students flexibility to specialise. Students carry out an independent research project and there is opportunity to undertake a four-week work placement. The BSc Cognitive Science is a recognised psychology degree in which psychology is integrated with the study of artificial intelligence, linguistics and philosophy. Students develop a broad range of research, technical and applied skills. The Psychology Department has a strong research record and a top rating for teaching quality.

Huddersfield University

University of Huddersfield, Queensgate, Huddersfield HD1 3DH
Tel: 01484 422288

This BSc in Psychology begins with introductory modules in psychology, sociology and social research methods. In the final year, there are optional psychology modules within the behavioural sciences area of the human and health sciences. The BSc in Psychology and Computing aims to integrate the two through practical applications. This degree provides students with the skills and knowledge to work in a computing profession that demands an understanding of human needs and contributions in technology. This gives students a competitive edge in jobs relating to Information Technology.

Hull University

University of Hull, Hull HU6 7RX
Tel: 01482 46311

This is a three-year BSc in Psychology course that is hierarchically organised into levels arranged so that in the first year you will receive a broad introduction to psychology and in subsequent years modules become more specialised and advanced. Hull also offers a four-year Psychology with Occupational Psychology, a three-year Psychology with Counselling Psychology, and joint Honours degrees combining Psychology with Sociology, Anthropology or Philosophy. These joint courses last for three years and students spend approximately 70% of their study on psychology components and 30% on their other subject. There is also direct entry to postgraduate clinical psychology training from the psychology courses.

Keele University

The University, Keele, Staffordshire ST5 5BG
Tel: 01782 621111

Students combine psychology with another subject following a dual

Honours degree programme in addition to a one-year subsidiary course in a third subject. Combinations are wide and range from American Studies to Statistics. Criminology is the most popular subject followed by English, neuroscience and law. A modular system is followed where all students take two modules per semester. Students can spend a semester at one of Keele's North American partner institutions, eg Brock University in Canada. The department has particular strengths in learning disability, social development, cognition and perception, health psychology and music psychology.

Kent University

University of Kent at Canterbury, Kent CT2 7NZ
Tel: 01227 764000

Kent offers degrees in Psychology, Social Psychology, Social Psychology with Clinical Psychology, Applied Psychology, Applied Social Psychology with Clinical Psychology and European Social Psychology. There is the opportunity to spend a year at a European university under the Psychology and European Social Psychology courses. Four-year degrees include a placement where one undertakes special project work in the NHS, Prison Service or government research establishment.

King Alfred's CHE

King Alfred's College, Sparkford Road, Winchester, Hampshire SO22 4NR
Tel: 01962 841515

This is an accredited college of Southampton University but applications are made direct to the college. Psychology is offered as part of a combined Honours programme in which you take two subjects. After the first year, you may choose to study psychology as a main, equal or minor part of your degree. The main (75%) pathway into psychology is accredited by the BPS with GBR.

Kingston University

Kingston University, Penrhyn Road, Kingston upon Thames,
Surrey KT1 2EE
Tel: 0181 547 2000

Psychology is offered under a modular framework giving students considerable autonomy. Tutors are drawn from different faculties.

Lancaster University

Lancaster University, University House, Lancaster LA1 4YW
Tel: 01524 65201

People typically register for a BA or a BSc on the basis of what minor subjects they want to do. You take three subjects in your first year and then concentrate on psychology in the second and third year. A number of students are able to go on an American exchange scheme whereby the second year is spent at the University of Colorado or Iowa. Selection is partly dependent on academic results. The third year is then spent back at Lancaster University. There is also a variety of combined degrees. Those combining psychology with a foreign language do a four-year course with one year spent abroad. Specific combined degrees include Psychology and Organisation Studies, Educational Studies, Linguistics or Women's Studies.

La Sainte Union CHE

La Sainte Union College, The Avenue, Southampton,
Hampshire SO9 5HB
Tel: 01703 228761

This is an accredited college of Southampton University but applications are made direct to the college. Psychology is studied as a combined BA/BSc Honours under a modular scheme.

Leeds, Trinity & All Saints College

Leeds, Trinity & All Saints College, Brownberrie Lane, Horsforth, Leeds LS18 5HP
Tel: 0113 283 7123

Psychology is studied in combination with either management or media. The course focuses on behavioural, cognitive and humanistic approaches. Three pathways are specifically developed: health and wellbeing, occupational psychology and issues in psychology. Students who wish to pursue careers as professional psychologists should contact the college to check the course has been recognised by the BPS. In the final year, students have the opportunity to apply their skills and knowledge by conducting an individual research project. They then work in small groups suggesting solutions to practical real world problems presented in the form of case studies. Specialised options include: human machine interaction, health psychology, psychology of reasoning and decision making, mental health and the psychology of gender.

Leeds University

University of Leeds, Leeds LS2 9JT
Tel: 0113 233 5719

Psychology facilities include a suite of interview and group rooms, human factors and workplace laboratory, a driving simulator, a human nutrition laboratory, a multi-unit speech laboratory and a cognitive psychology laboratory. The department provides a common room for students and has an active staff/student liaison committee. The department offers six courses leading to a degree that grants GBR eligibility which include: BSc Psychology, BSc Applied Psychology (part-time), BA Psychology and Management Studies, BSc Psychology with Philosophy, History or Science, BA in Psychology and Sociology and a BSc Cognitive Science and BSc in Psychology and Neuroscience.The courses are split into modules and credits.

Leicester University

University of Leicester, University Road, Leicester LE1 7RH
Tel: 0116 252 2522

The headquarters of the BPS is situated in Leicester and maintains close links with the department. The research and teaching facilities include two large computer laboratories, a video laboratory, a psychometric test library and a music research library. Research strengths are concentrated in cognitive psychology, clinical psychology, legal psychology, social behaviour, development and neuroscience. A supplementary subject is taken in the first and second year with a choice of biological sciences, computer science, English, pure mathematics or sociology. A BSc in Psychology with Sociology is also offered and accepted by the BPS, of which two-thirds of the time is spent on psychology and a third on sociology.

Lincolnshire & Humberside University

Lincoln University Campus, Brayford Pool, Lincoln LN6 7TS
Tel: 01522 882000

There are two psychology programmes – the single Honours programme and the Psychology major. The latter is the programme followed in joint degrees. Psychology can be studied in combination with criminology, management, health studies, marketing and social policy. Both programmes cover the core areas of psychology supported by units on research design and methods, information technology, statistics and data analysis. On the single Honours programme, students have a wide choice of specialist topics to choose from in the final year.

Liverpool Hope University College

Liverpool Hope University College, Hope Park,
Liverpool L16 9JD
Tel: 0151 291 3000

An approved BPS programme, psychology is offered within the BA/BSc combined modular degree. A wide variety of final year options are offered including crime, peace, organisational, counselling, ecopsychology and parapsychology. Facilities within the department include observation and perception laboratories. Hope has a commitment to provide a quality learning experience for all students and, to enhance this, the department has an active staff/student committee. The main Hope campus is located in a leafy suburb, a few miles from the city centre. Liverpool Hope is an accredited college of the University of Liverpool.

Liverpool John Moores University

Liverpool John Moores University, Roscoe Court,
4 Rodney Street, Liverpool L1 2TZ
Tel: 0151 231 5090

This BSc Applied Psychology operates within an Integrated Credit Scheme (ICS) which allows for a full scale of awards ranging from single subjects to joint, combined Honours and Diplomas and Certificates. Specialisation can be delayed until level 2.

Liverpool University

The University of Liverpool, Eleanor Rathbone Building,
Bedford Street, South, Liverpool L69 7ZA
Tel:0151 794 2957

In addition to the main BSc (Hons) Psychology with about 80 places, there are 30 places each in two new courses starting in 1999 – BSc (Hons) Psychology and Neuroscience and BSc (Hons) Psychology and Health Sciences. Each of these courses will have at its core the main fields and methods in psychology which have consistently conferred upon the principal Honours course the BPS's recognition as a route to higher degrees in research and applied psychology. A virtual doubling of staff numbers will provide tuition not only through lectures and tutorials but also via interactive experimental work, mainly in individual and small group projects.

London, Goldsmiths

Goldsmiths College, University of London, London SE14 6NW
Tel: 0171 919 7171

This is a three-year course in which the final year offers a higher level of specialisation in selected topics including occupational psychology, cognitive psychology, neuropsychology, social psychology, psycho-pharmacology, psychology of consciousness and psychopathology. Opportunities for part-time study and intercalated work programmes are available within the BSc programme.

London, Guildhall

London Guildhall University, 133 Whitechapel High Street, London E1 7QA
Tel: 0171 320 1616

This BSc Psychology degree is concentrated within the Department's centre for Behavioural Neuroscience and the Centre for Applied Cognitive Psychology. The degree also has the advantage of being recognised by The Ergonomics Society.

London, LSE

London School of Economics & Political Science,
University of London, Houghton Street, London WC2A 2AS
Tel: 0171 955 7124

The first Chair of Social Psychology at a UK university was established at the London School of Economics in 1964 when the Department of Social Psychology was founded. Today, it is the largest department of Social Psychology in Europe. There are links with other centres of social psychology in Central and Eastern Europe, the Middle East, the Pacific and the Americas. There are opportunities to study a BSc in Psychology and Philosophy which gives a unique perspective on social and cognitive psychology by integrating it with the philosophical dimension. Alternatively there is a BSc in Social Policy with Social Psychology where psychology topics are applied to wider issues of policy and the social structure.

London, Royal Holloway

Royal Holloway, University of London, Egham Hill,
Egham, Surrey TW20 0EX
Tel: 01784 434455

The Psychology Department has links with hospitals, schools and businesses which can be especially useful for the experimental projects carried out in the second and third years. There is a newly built teaching laboratory and good facilities such as psychological recording and closed circuit TV and radio. The single Honours BSc Psychology leads to GBR but the joint Honours combining Psychology with Mathematics or Music does not lead to GBR. The status of the joint degree scheme is currently under review but any potential student who is contemplating a career in psychology is advised to apply for the single Honours degree.

London, University College

UCL, Gower Street, London WC1E 6BT
Tel: 0171 387 7050

One of the first British laboratories in Experimental Psychology was established at UCL in 1897 and it was here in 1901 that the BPS was inaugurated. The department is now the largest Department of Psychology in the UK and is a major centre for psychological research with strengths in vision, cognition, neuropsychology and clinical psychology. Its experimental work is supported by three research councils and many other research-oriented bodies. During the first two years, students study all aspects of the subject and may also choose subsidiary course units from outside the department. Laboratory work in the second year involves students designing and conducting their own experiments in small groups which provides a basis for the final year project. In the final year, in addition to the compulsory research project, students may study a variety of courses such as occupational psychology, language and cognition, visual perception, social psychology, theory of mind, etc. The department also offers Psychology with Cognitive Science which provides a more interdisciplinary stream of study that investigates the mental processes through experimental research and computer modelling. All candidates to whom places are offered are interviewed (overseas applicants excepted).

Loughborough University

Loughborough University, Loughborough, Leicestershire LE11 3TU
Tel: 01509 263171

The Department of Social Sciences includes Social Psychology. The department has links with the Centre for Research in Social Policy (CRSP), the Communications Research Centre and the Midland's Centre for Criminology and Criminal Justice.

Luton University

Luton University, Park Square, Luton, Bedfordshire LU1 3JU
Tel: 01582 734111

Luton operates a modular system and offers single, major and joint modes of study. If prescribed pathways are followed, the degree may be recognised by the BPS for GBR eligibility.

Manchester Metropolitan University

Manchester Metropolitan University, All Saints, Manchester M15 6BH
Tel: 0161 247 2000

The department offers a unique range of courses, providing a comprehensive and integrated study of the fundamental areas of the discipline, and the opportunity to specialise. All courses listed here are BPS recognised as providing the GBR. The major course is the three-year BSc degree course in Psychology with the opportunity for named routes (in, for instance, criminology). There is also a combined Honours degree, allowing psychology to be studied as a major along with a wide range of other subjects. There is also a four-year degree in Psychology and Speech Pathology, which is recognised also by the Royal College of Speech and Language Therapists, thereby providing graduates with a dual qualification. Opportunities exist for part of the course to be spent elsewhere in Europe, Australia or the USA.

Manchester University

University of Manchester, Oxford Road, Manchester M13 9PL
Tel: 0161 275 2077

The department was established in 1919 and was the first in Great Britain to appoint a full-time Professor of Psychology. The majority of students work towards a BA or BSc Psychology degree that consists of three years. There are no differences between the two courses and the two titles only exist due to historical reasons. There is also a joint degree in Psychology and Neuroscience. The neuroscience element covers a range of relevant biological topics as well as neurobiology. Psychology may be studied as an option as part of the BA combined studies in Art or BA in Human Communication but these are not recognised by the BPS. The department takes part in the ERASMUS programme. This scheme brings under-graduates from psychology departments of various European universities together therefore allowing good students with relevant language abilities to spend a year at another university.

Middlesex University

Middlesex University, White Hart Lane, London N17 8HR
Tel: 0181 362 5000

The Psychology degree at Middlesex was one of the first to be recognised by the BPS. Formats of study include a specialised degree, a major or a minor subject. There is the option of work placements in advertising, mental health, the police and Crown Prosecution Service and other academic research departments. There is also a BA in Psychology and Spanish with the first semester of the final year being spent studying psychology at Bilbao University, Spain.

Newcastle University

University of Newcastle upon Tyne, 6 Kensington Terrace,
Newcastle upon Tyne NE1 7RU
Tel: 0191 222 6000

Newcastle offers Psychology as a BSc or a BA. There is also the option of combining psychology with speech, computing science, mathematics or science. The department works closely together with neuroscience and zoology.

North East Wales Institute of Higher Education

North East Wales Institute (NEWI), Plas Coch, Mold Road, Wrexham, Clwyd LL11 2AW
Tel: 01978 290666

The NEWI offers a BSc Psychology course. It is a single modular degree which is currently seeking BPS recognition.

North London University

University of North London, 166–220 Holloway Road, London N7 8DB
Tel: 0171 607 2789

The Psychology programme includes modules from the School of Life Sciences, Computing and Engineering. Combinations include a wide variety ranging from communications and cultural studies to marketing.

Northampton University College

UCN, Broughton Green Road, Northampton NN2 7AL
Tel: 01604 735500

Students at UCN can study psychology as a single Honours subject, or as part of a combined Honours subject, or as part of a combined Honours programme which enables them to study psychology as a major, minor or joint subject. Empirical investigation is integral to all the psychology courses, and there is progression through each degree towards specialist final year options. These include clinical psychology, parapyschology, forensic psychology and neuropsychology. Students who have followed specified pathways are eligible to apply for GBR with the BPS.

Northumbria University

University of Northumbria at Newcastle, Ellison Building
Ellison Place, Newcastle upon Tyne NE1 8ST
Tel: 0191 232 6002

The Psychology degree has a substantial practical component and includes basic training in research methods, supervised practical classes, training in the use of standardised tests and a substantial final year research project. It is also possible to study psychology in combination with either sport science or computing. All these degrees are recognised by the BPS as conferring the GBR as a Chartered Psychologist.

Nottingham Trent University

Nottingham Trent University, Burton Street, Nottingham NG1 4BU
Tel: 0115 941 8418

The Psychology degree is located in the Department of Applied Social Studies which covers areas of health, social work and criminology. There is also the option of studying a BA in Social Science if you are unsure of whether or not to take psychology as a single Honours.

Nottingham University

University of Nottingham, University Park, Nottingham NG7 2RD
Tel: 0115 951 5151

The School of Psychology is one of the largest and strongest in the country with excellent laboratories and IT facilities. There are leading research groups in developmental psychology, cognition and cognitive neuropsychology and in computational modelling. The first and second year contain all the compulsory core modules for BPS recognition, enabling finalists to concentrate on areas of interest. Practical and statistical modules are taken in the first two years to prepare for the third year project which accounts for one third of the final-year grade. All students register for a BSc degree, although applicants with arts and humanities A-levels, or a mixture, are encouraged to apply. Students take different subsidiary modules in their first year depending on their background. There is a joint Honours programme with Philosophy.

Oxford Brookes University

Oxford Brookes University, Gipsy Lane, Headington, Oxford OX3 0BP
Tel: 01865 741111

Within the School of Social Sciences and Law, Psychology is a three-year BA/BSc course studied as a joint degree with one from over 60 other subjects from across the university. It is possible to change to a single Honours course after the first year. The department recently received an 'Excellent' quality assurance rating. The course is modular and emphasises practical and laboratory experience. A range of assessments is used including seminars, coursework and examinations. With an appropriate course of study, students obtain GBR. The department also offers a one-year conversion course to the GBR for non-Psychology graduates.

Oxford University

University of Oxford, Admissions Office, Wellington Square,
Oxford OX1 2JD
Tel: 01865 270000

You can study Psychology at Oxford in two ways: either as a part subject in the joint Honours School with Philosophy or Physiology, or as a subject on its own in Experimental Psychology. Decisions on selection are made by the individual colleges, not by the Department of Experimental Psychology. You should choose a college which has a tutor in psychology (not available at Mansfield, Merton, St Peters or Trinity). The first two terms consist of three introductory courses. You will then be examined at the end of your second term (an examination called Prelims) which allows you to commence work on your finals.

Paisley University

University of Paisley, Paisley PA1 2BE
Tel: 0141 848 3000

The Behavioural Sciences programme can be taken over three years for a BA or four years for a BA Honours. The programme helps students use the findings, theories and methods of psychology to explore and understand life in contemporary society. In the final year you can choose 'elective' modules from across the university, in addition to the core elements of the programme. Paisley offers a comprehensive personal tutorial system and provides courses geared towards specific careers or postgraduate study. The degree is recognised by the BPS as conferring Graduate Basis for Registration.

Plymouth University

University of Plymouth, Drake Circus, Plymouth PL4 8AA
Tel: 01752 600600

There are opportunities to study Psychology as a single or joint degree and to obtain work experience under two different routes. The first way is through the Visits Programme in which students attend an organisation that does work relevant to psychology. Attendance is for one half-day per week for one semester. This programme is the first of its kind in the UK. The second route is through a Sandwich Placement year. Successful completion of the year entitles you to the Certificate of Industrial and Professional Experience.

Portsmouth University

University of Portsmouth, Winston Churchill Avenue,
Portsmouth PO1 2UP
Tel: 01705 876543

The Department of Psychology offers a single Honours BSc in Psychology which is delivered over three years with two semesters per year. The course emphasises a 'hands-on' approach to psychology and encourages links with ongoing staff research. Departmental research interests include police interviewing, reliability of child witnesses, developmental disabilities, the social construction of disability, infant development, the development of number, colour perception, speech perception, intentionality, neuropsychology, ergonomics, deception, locomotion and consciousness. The department has a well-equipped teaching and laboratory facilities.

Queen Margaret College

Queen Margaret College, Clerwood Terrace, Edinburgh EH12 8TS
Tel: 0131 317 3000

The college is situated in Edinburgh and is a university sector institution. Psychology is offered as a major/joint/minor or as an option in the BSc Social Sciences and Health course.

Reading University

The University of Reading, Whiteknights, Reading RG6 6AH
Tel: 0118 987 5123

The single Honours degree in Psychology is available through the Faculty of Science and leads to a BSc qualification. During the first year students study other subjects of their choice alongside psychology; during year 2 they follow core courses in psychology, progressing into more specialised and independent study in the third year. Psychology may be combined with sociology, philosophy, linguistics or art in the Faculty of Letters and Social Sciences, or with physiology, zoology, mathematics or statistics in the Faculty of Science. The single Honours degree and all joint degrees are accredited as conferring eligibility for Graduate Membership of the BPS and giving the GBR which is the first step to becoming a Chartered Psychologist.

Ripon and York College

College of Ripon and York, Lord Mayor's Walk, York YO31 7EX
Tel: 01904 656771

Psychology is available as a new specialist single Honours degree from September 1999. The tutors have backgrounds in Applied Psychology and are dedicated to teaching and research in psychology. Psychology is also available as a minor subject in a combined Honours programme with PE, Language Studies and Social Science.

Roehampton Institute, London

Roehampton Institute London, Roehampton Lane, London SW15 5PU
Tel: 0181 392 3000

A BSc in Psychology and Counselling is offered here and is the only one of its kind in Britain. You will learn basic counselling skills and participate in personal growth work as well as psychology. It has links with a number of hospitals, counselling centres and universities. There is also a BA/BSc Combined Degree Programme.

St Andrews University

University of St Andrews, College Gate, St Andrews, Fife KY16 9AJ
Tel: 01334 476161

Psychology may be taken as a first year subject in either the Arts or Sciences. A more advanced course can be taken in the second year and students who do well in this can go on to take the two-year Honours Psychology degree course either as a single subject or jointly with one of a wide range of alternatives.

Sheffield Hallam University

Sheffield Hallam University, Howard Street, Sheffield S1 1WB
Tel: 0114 272 0911

Psychology is located in the School of Health and Community Studies under an Applied Social Studies Honours degree programme. One of the main features is its international focus; it has links with other European countries so studying overseas is an option.

Sheffield University

University of Sheffield, Western Bank, Sheffield S10 2TN
Tel: 0114 276 8555

The Psychology Department is attached to two research units of international importance: the Artificial Intelligence and Vision Research Unit, and the Institute of Work Psychology. Most courses are modular and students must pass a number of modules in their subject of study as well as units from other courses. Dual subjects combining psychology with philosophy or sociology may be taken in the Faculty of Social Sciences.

South Bank University

South Bank University, 103 Borough Road, London SE1 0AA
Tel: 0171 928 8989

The Psychology Division in the Faculty of Humanities and Social Sciences is an expanding unit which is active in research. Interests include speech and language difficulties, developmental psychology, social psychology, cross-cultural psychology and cognitive psychology. South Bank offers Psychology as a single Honours or combined Honours degree programme. Students on the single Honours programme study core areas of Psychology during their first two years and select a range of specialist Psychology options in their third year. Combined Honours Psychology may be studied with any one of a wide range of other fields, including criminal studies, in a minor/joint/major structure. All psychology courses, except the minor, are currently recognised by the BPS as conferring the GBR.

Southampton Institute

Southampton Institute, East Park Terrace, Southampton SO14 0YN
Tel: 01703 319000

The Social Science Faculty has offered a single Honours BSc in Psychology since 1996. The focus of the course is the study of mind and behaviour with coverage of the major topic areas within the field of psychology (biological, cognitive, social, developmental and individual differences approaches) as well as research methodology, quantitative and qualitative analysis and some related disciplines such as sociology. There is an emphasis throughout the course, and especially within the third year, on the application of psychology to real world issues.

Southampton University

University of Southampton, Highfield, Southampton SO17 1BJ
Tel: 01703 595000

The Psychology Department has three research groupings in Health and Community Psychology, Development and Learning, and Cognitive Psychology. Students may study a single Honours Bsc in Psychology or a combined Honours BSc Psychology with Physiology. Candidates interested in the latter degree are recommended to have studied Chemistry to at least GCSE level and Biology to A-level.

Staffordshire University

Staffordshire University, College Road, Stoke-on-Trent ST4 2DE
Tel: 01782 294643

A single Honours Psychology programme is offered, as well as combined Honours Psychology with other subjects and an Honours degree in Psychology and Criminology. All programmes are approved as giving the GBR. Psychology at Stafford has received an 'Excellent' assessment for its educational provision from the Quality Assurance Agency for Higher Education – scoring maximum grades in five of six categories. The courses offer a very wide range of applied psychology options in the final year of study. Staff are active in research across many different fields of psychology.

Stirling University

The University of Stirling, Stirling FK9 4LA
Tel: 01786 473171

At the University of Stirling the approach to psychology is an empirical one. An emphasis is placed on practical work from the beginning of year 1. Combined degree programmes are available across a range of disciplines (currently 13 in total). Both single and combined Honours students are automatically eligible for graduate registration with the BPS. A wide range of study electives are available, spanning neuropsychology, social and educational psychology, and community psychology. The department took part in the Teaching Quality Assessment in autumn 1997 and was rated 'Excellent'.

Strathclyde University

University of Strathclyde, Richmond Street, Glasgow G1 1XQ
Tel: 0141 552 4400

In the first year, psychology may be chosen as one of five subjects selected from a broad range of classes in Arts, Social Sciences and Business Studies. Students can then choose psychology and one other subject and continue their study in second and third year. In the fourth year psychology may be studied to single or joint Honours levels. Admission to psychology classes in both second year and Honours year is selective. The department has particular strengths in the areas of social psychology, developmental and educational psychology, occupational and health psychology, perceptual-motor skills, neuropsychology, psychology of language and human communication, psychology and C&IT, interactive learning, and road-user behaviour.

Sunderland University

University of Sunderland, Edinburgh Building, Chester Road, Sunderland SR1 3SD
Tel: 0191 515 2000

This is a three-year BSc degree in which one-year exchanges to the US, France, Germany, Ireland, Spain, Crete and Finland are available.

Surrey University

University of Surrey, Guildford GU2 5XH
Tel: 01483 300800

This is a four-year course in which the third year is organised around a period of professional placements so that the students have direct experience of the practical applications of psychology. It enables them to bring this experience back to the university and apply it to final year studies. There are also extensive international links with the United States or as an ERASMUS student in France, Italy or Spain. Surrey also offers a four-year BSc in Applied Psychology and Sociology that stresses the integration of theory to practice whether it be industry, urban development, social welfare, health or education.

Sussex University

University of Sussex, Falmer, Brighton, Sussex BN1 9RH
Tel: 01273 678416

There is the choice of a BA in Applied Psychology where there is an emphasis on applying psychology to practical problems, a BA in Developmental Psychology, a BSc in Sociology and Social Psychology as well as the normal BA or BSc in Psychology. There are many courses on offer and links with the Cognitive Science Department.

Teesside University

University of Teesside, Middlesbrough, Cleveland TS1 3BA
Tel: 01642 218121

This three-year BSc course places an emphasis on 'hands on' research experience through laboratory research classes. Core modules include foundations of psychology, biopsychology, perception, cognitive psychology, social psychology and developmental psychology.

Thames Valley University

Thames Valley University, St Mary's Road, Ealing, London W5 5RF
Tel: 0181 231 2902

Thames Valley offers a BSc in Psychology, a BSc in Health and Community Psychology, and a BSc in Psychology and Counselling Theory. Students take the same modules in the first two years after which they have the option of progressing to one of the three Honours routes. In the second year, all students have a placement allowing them to gain experience within a research, industrial, health or community setting.

Ulster University

University of Ulster, Cromore Road, Coleraine, County Londonderry, Northern Ireland BT52 1SA
Tel: 01265 44141

Ulster offers a course in BSc Applied Psychology with an 18-week work placement in the third year. Students may spend their placement outside of Northern Ireland. The majority of placements are located in Great Britain and the Republic of Ireland. Ulster also offers a BSc in Social Psychology, a BSc in Psychology and Organisational Science, and a BSc in Social Psychology and Sociology, all with short periods of work placements.

Wales (Bangor)

The University of Wales, Bangor, Gwynedd LL57 3DG
Tel: 01248 351151

The most recent official assessments of research and teaching showed the School of Psychology at Bangor to be among the leading departments in the country. Facilities include a Student Learning Resource Centre, a Macintosh Laboratory with 80 machines for student use, and a day nursery in which child behaviour can be observed first hand. Teaching is carried out in a flexible and student-orientated manner, supported by the latest technology. Areas of research include learning language and development, cognitive psychology and neuroscience, clinical and health psychology and experimental consumer psychology. Undergraduates take a BA or BSc degree (with no difference in course content) and may read for Honours in either Psychology or Psychology with Health Psychology.

Wales (Cardiff)

Cardiff University, PO Box 921, Cardiff CF1 3XQ
Tel: 01222 874000

Cardiff receives research grants from the major research councils, the Home Office, the Ministry of Defence, the Health and Safety Executive, the Wellcome Foundation as well as industry. The BA and

BSc courses are essentially the same. If you are taking a four-year Applied Psychology degree, you spend 12 months in a professional placement approved by the department. The degree in Applied Psychology confers membership of the Society's Division of Occupational Psychology and a reduction in the postgraduate period before Chartered Status may be confirmed. There are joint Honours in Psychology with Sociology, Physiology and Humanities.

University of Wales Institute Cardiff

UWIC, Llandaff Campus, Western Avenue, Cardiff CF5 2YB;
Tel 01222 506070

UWIC offers a BSc (Hons) Psychology, a BSc (Hons) Psychology and Communication, and a BSc (Hons) Psychology with Nutrition. All psychology students take a common first year, introducing them to the core psychology subjects which are developed over the next two years. The specialist subjects for the psychology, communication and nutrition routes are studied in the second and third years. Psychology at UWIC underwent an assessment by the Higher Education Funding Council for Wales recently, and was awarded the highest possible rating of 'Excellent'. All three degrees are recognised by the BPS as conferring GBR as a Chartered Psychologist.

Wales (Swansea)

University of Wales, Swansea, Singleton Park, Swansea SA2 8PP
Tel: 01792 205678

Psychology at Swansea can be studied as a single subject or as a pair of subjects in the Faculty of Arts and Social Studies or Sciences. Joint Honours include Psychology with Sociology, Social Anthropology, Economics, Philosophy, Biology and Computer Science.

Warwick University

University of Warwick, Coventry CV4 7AL
Tel: 01203 523523

Warwick offers a single Honours degree in Psychology and joint degrees in Psychology with Education or Philosophy. The combination of Psychology with Education is of practical value as the two interact. The study of learning and intelligence involves an input from both areas. This course provides good preparation for those who intend to enter the education profession or social services.

Westminster University

University of Westminster, 309 Regent Street, London W1R 8AL
Tel: 0171 911 5000

BSc Psychology is a single Honours degree offered on the Regent Street Campus in central London. Core areas such as social and developmental psychology, personality and research design and analysis are studied in the first and second year with the choice of more applied areas in year three including forensic, business, educational, clinical and counselling psychology. The degree may be taken part-time and many modules also run in the evening. The University also offers a BSc in Psychological Sciences and a BSc in Cognitive Sciences. All three degrees are accredited for Graduate Basis for Registration of BPS.

Wolverhampton University

The University of Wolverhampton, Wulfruna Street, Wolverhampton WV1 1SB Tel: 01902 321000

Wolverhampton offers a three-year BSc Psychology degree that aims to provide a comprehensive package of psychology which develops your skills as an independent learner and critical thinker. Psychology may be studied as a major, joint or minor in combination with other science and technology subjects in the BSc Applied Sciences. The optional sandwich year allows some students to extend their studies to four years.

Worcester University College

University College Worcester, Henwick Grove, Worcester WR2 6AJ
Tel: 01905 855000

Students may follow either a single Honours, major, joint or minor pathway in Psychology. Those graduating with a single, major or joint degree will be eligible to apply for Graduate Membership of the BPS. Those who follow a specified route through the single Honours pathway will be eligible to apply for Graduate Membership with GBR of the BPS. Psychology combines well with health studies, business management, biological science, sociology and education studies. The department has specific research interests in the areas of social psychology, occupational psychology, developmental psychology and gerontology and offers an MSc in Gerontology. Others Masters courses are currently being developed.

University of York

The University, Heslington, York YO1 5DD
Tel: 01904 430000

This is a single subject course with the choice of whether to gain a BA or BSc being decided in the final year subject to the approval of the Board of Studies. The Language for All Programme (LFA) offers you the opportunity to take a foreign language course alongside your main subject of study.

FURTHER INFORMATION & READING LIST

BRITISH PSYCHOLOGICAL SOCIETY

The British Psychological Society is the professional association for Psychologists and is incorporated by Royal Charter. A Register of Chartered Psychologists was established in 1987, bringing a more organised and stricter discipline to the profession. Chartered Psychologists are bound to an ethical code of conduct which was set up to maintain the standards of psychology as a profession and to protect the public.

The Register contains members of the Society who have reached a certain standard in education and work experience. It contains their names, qualifications and work addresses. Copies of the Register can be found at main public reference libraries and at professional organisations and certain employer bodies.

The Register is split into specialist areas such as Clinical, Criminological and Legal, Educational, Occupational and Counselling Psychology.

To qualify for registration as a Chartered Psychologist you must:

- have completed a first qualification in psychology that is a Graduate Basis for Registration;
- have undergone a further course or supervised training in a specific area of psychology;
- have agreed to abide by a Code of Conduct laid down by the British Psychology Society;
- be judged fit to practise psychology without supervision.

For further information contact: The British Psychological Society, St Andrews House, 48 Princess Road East, Leicester LE1 7DR.

GENERAL UNIVERSITY GUIDES

The UCAS Handbook is free to UK addresses from UCAS, PO Box 28, Cheltenham, Gloucestershire GL52 3LZ.

University and College Entrance: The Official Guide, published by UCAS and available from Sheed & Ward Ltd, 14 Coopers Row, London EC3 2BH.

Entrance Guide to Higher Education in Scotland, published by the Committee of Scottish Higher Education Principals, St Andrew House, 141 West Hill Street, Glasgow G1 2RN.

CRAC Degree Course Guides (Psychology), by Sophie Harper, published by Hobsons Publishing. Enquiries for catalogue to: Hobsons Publishing plc, Bateman Street, Cambridge CB2 1LZ. Orders to: Biblios Publishers' Distribution Ltd, Star Road, Partridge Green, West Sussex RH1 8LD; Tel: 0403 710851.

How to Complete Your UCAS Form, published annually by Trotman & Co Ltd, 2 The Green, Richmond, Surrey TW9 1PL.

The Complete Degree Course Offers, by Brian Heap, published annually by Trotman & Co Ltd.

The NatWest Student Book, Klaus Boehm & Jenny Lees-Spalding (eds), published annually by Trotman & Co Ltd.

PSYCHOLOGY TEXTS

As far as specific psychology textbooks go, any of the introductory texts found in large bookshops are fine. Those relating to Social Psychology are probably the easiest and most interesting to read if you are new to the subject. You might like to dip into one or more of the following:

The Social Animal, by Elliot Aronson, published by Freeman.

Readings about the Social Animal, by Elliot Aronson, published by Freeman. This is a good book to read in conjunction with The Social Animal and describes actual experiments/studies carried out, giving details on the methods used, the results and the conclusions drawn.

Social Psychology: Understanding Human Interaction, by Robert Bacon & Donn Byrne, published by Allyn & Bacon.